My Life as a Kid

20-Year Anniversary Edition Collection

Written and Illustrated by:

CHESSON

Foreword Contributed by:
CLINT FISHER

No part of this publication may be reproduced, stored in a retrieval system, or transmitted in any form or by any means, electronic, mechanical, photocopying, recording, or otherwise, without written permission by Miss Birdie's Books, Inc.

ISBN:
 978-0-999-28379-0
Copyright 1998, 2018 by Birdie Chesson
Copyright 2018 by Birdie Chesson,
Foreword by Clint Fisher L.P.C.

All rights reserved. Published by Miss Birdie's Books, Inc. and associated logos are trademarks and/or registered under Miss Birdie's Books, Inc.

My Life As a Kid Collection is registered under MBB, Inc. Printed in the U.S.A.

My Life as a Kid Collection

5	Foreword
10	Pick on me
19	Lacey
39	Mom is Sick
48	No Time
58	Earl
74	Strangers
89	You Are So Special To Me
98	My Friend Mario
109	What is Under my Clothes?
126	About My Life as a Kid

My Life As A Kid

Foreword
By Clint Fisher, L.P.C.

There is a lot that goes into the various discussions with our kids nowadays. Sometimes the kids bring things up in awkward places or the subject matter is something they are developmentally not able to grasp. How do we navigate these times?

Children have a way of constantly surprising us, over and over and over again. There is no perfect answer, no "Master Key" response that will always work. Throughout my career of working with young children, I have found two ways to respond that seem to take the edge off.

Let's first ask, "Why do kids say the things they say?" Usually, they are genuinely asking a question to better understand a situation. This situation could be one they are in or one they observe. They may see something that does not make sense to them and try to find a way to explain it.

This search sometimes brings them to one, or many questions and to why they turn to adults for the answers in the first place.

Just because a child asks a question that may be 'off color' or 'socially unacceptable' does not mean that they are trying to be mean. I feel strongly that it is in fact the exact *opposite*. They are trying to make sense of what they are seeing. In these potentially awkward times, the best response is to both validate and normalize their thoughts and words.

By validating the child's thoughts, you are communicating in a simple way that the child is important and their questions are valid. Here is an example of something that I witnessed in a coffee shop in my neighborhood.

To set the stage, I live in New York City. In such a huge city, you become almost immune to visual stimulus; although every once and awhile, even adults, see things that catch them off guard. I was standing behind a young mother and her daughter as we waited for our coffee order.

The front door opened and an individual entered wearing a dress. I can see why this might have been confusing to the little girl as the individual also had a full beard and mustache. The little girl tugged on her mom's shirt and then loudly asked why that man was dressed up like Halloween. The mom got down on her knees and in a quiet voice talked with her daughter.

She started with, *"I can understand why that would be confusing to you but remember that we do not point anyone out by how they are dressed or what they look like"*. She went on to make a few points about how everyone has the right to dress and act how they want to and the only person we are worried about is...... (she waited for her daughter to fill in the blank), OURSELVES.

Let's talk more about this at home. This is a wonderful example of the mom honored the girl's question and took a moment to validate and normalize what she was asking about.

While the mom could have frozen in embarrassment, she chose to make the moment a teachable moment and put her daughter's curiosity in the forefront.

Normalization and validation are two simple concepts that set the stage for a great deal of candid, deep and meaningful discussions where you can truly connect with your child. Some conversations may be more difficult, some may not even end well; but having an open, trusting relationship where your child feel safe enough to ask in today's changing world is exactly what you WANT. If they do not ask you, they ***will*** find out another way.

This book is a great way to "set the stage" some of the 'tough' discussions. If you have a difficult time connecting with your child, Birdie Chesson has helped you tremendously through her writing, the children's stories (based on real children) within this collection.

Read it yourself, and make notes in the margins and then read it with your kids. Take the time to invest in your children, even when the conversations are difficult!

The connection that is created through conversation is the strongest one.

My Life As A Kid

WHY DO THEY PICK ON ME?

A "Talk To Me" Series Book
By Birdie Chesson

WHY DO THEY PICK ON ME?

A "Talk To Me" Series Book
Written and Illustrated by Birdie Chesson

Why do people pick on me?
It seems like they are always trying
to make me cry.
They hurt my feelings and try to make
me feel bad about myself.
Sometimes the kids at school make fun of
me.
Sometimes it is kids in my neighborhood.
Sometimes it is some of my family that are
mean to me.

Sometimes I wonder if they
feel good about
making me cry.

When I think about why they
treat me that way,
it makes me want to hide.

I still can't
understand why
they do it.

My grandma says that people see that I'm special and something inside of them wants to be like me.

But instead of trying to be my friend, they pick on me.
To me, that is still no reason to hurt me.
I wonder sometimes if it's what I do have that makes me so special.

I don't want to change anything about myself.
I'm special and I love who I am.
Grandma says for me to always be myself. To just be proud to be me.
So if they can't appreciate me, I have to keep whatever it is that makes me special, precious to myself.

I know that I have people that care about me and love me.

People that I can talk to about how I feel.

I want to make new friends and feel better about myself.

I love who I am.

So I will keep doing all of the good things that I like to do and make me happy.

I know that one day things will change.

I know that I am special and I am a good friend.

If people keep picking on me,
they will not get to know that about me.

And it will be *their* loss.

Not mine.

My Life As A Kid

Lacey

Lacey

A "Talk To Me" Series book
Written and Illustrated by Birdie Chesson

There is a girl in my class named Lacey.
I have known her since Kindergarten.

She is very quiet, very nice and I like her.

**But there's one thing that I don't understand.
Sometimes she wears long sleeved shirts and long pants…
Even in the summer!**

I thought that it was silly that she wore so many clothes because it gets so hot and she ends up sweating a lot.

Some of the other kids make fun of her for it.

We were in gym one day and I saw marks on Lacey's arm. They were bluish green and looked like fingers.

Our gym teacher, Ms. Lopez saw them too and asked her, "What happened to your arm, Lacey?"

"I was playing with my brother and I fell. It was an accident." she said. Ms. Lopez said,"Well, those are really bad bruises. Did you see a doctor for it?"

"My mom took care of it, Ms. Lopez."
"Ok, you have to be careful, Lacey.
I worry about you." "Yes, Ms. Lopez."
As our teacher walked away, Lacey looked so sad.

One day, she came to school wearing a cast on her arm.

I was shocked. I asked, "Lacey! What happened to your arm?" She put her head down. "Um, I fell." She said.

Then I remembered how many times I used to see marks and scars on Lacey's arms and legs.

**She always told everyone that she fell or she was playing rough. I started to think that she falls a lot.
But is she was telling the truth?**

"Lacey, did you really fall again and break your arm? We are friends, Lacey. *You can tell me.*" I told her.

Lacey started to cry. She whispered, "You have to promise me that you won't tell. I'll get in trouble."

She told me that her mother got really mad at her. She hit and grabbed Lacey so hard, she broke Lacey's arm.

I asked, "Does she hurt you a lot, Lacey?"

"Yes, but if I tell, it will get worse."

I was really scared for Lacey.

"So when our teacher saw your arm, was it really your brother that hurt you?"

"No." she said.

Even though I promised Lacey I wouldn't tell, I didn't want her to keep being hurt.

I didn't want her mad at me but I knew that I had to do the right thing.

When I saw Ms. Lopez the next day, I asked her if she and I could talk.

"Is there a problem?" She asked.

I asked, "If I know someone that is getting hurt, and they tell me not to tell, what should I do?"

She looked me in the eyes.
"If someone you know is being hurt, you *have* to tell because it *will* get worse."

I began to cry.
"Lacey is getting hurt at home and it *is* getting worse."

She said, "You are very brave. Telling me makes you a good friend."

"But what will happen to Lacey?"

"I'm going to call someone to help Lacey." she said.

I got worried. "Do you think that she will be mad at me for telling?"

"I think that one day, Lacey will understand that you cared about her so much that you told someone so that she could get help." said Ms. Lopez.

Lacey didn't come back to school after that day. I was so scared because I did not know what happened to her.

And I knew that she was gone because I told.

One day, I got a phone call.
It was Lacey.

I thought that I would never hear from her again.

I was so happy to hear from her.

I thought that she would be mad at me for telling her secret, but she wasn't. Lacey was very happy to hear from me.

She lives with her grandmother and she likes her new school.

I miss Lacey very much.

But I'm proud that I told someone that could help her that she was being hurt.

Now I know that I was being a good friend and keeping that bad secret would have hurt Lacey even more.

Now I don't have to worry about her being hurt anymore.
And that makes me feel good.

My Life As A Kid

Mom is Sick...

Written and Illustrated by
Birdie Chesson
A "Talk To Me" Series Book

Mom is Sick...

Written and Illustrated
by Birdie Chesson
A "Talk To Me" Series Book

My Dad and I went to the doctor's office today with my Mother.

My Mom had to stay in the hospital.

When my Dad and I came home, I saw that my Dad was very sad.

I have never seen his face look like that before.

I was worried about both of my parents.

I saw that my Dad was very sad.

My Dad tells me that my Mom is very sick.

Looking at his face I know that it is very bad.

That makes me scared.

I feel sad but I want my Mom and Dad to know that I can be a big kid.

I know that I am strong.

My Mom is in a lot of pain.
I know that I cannot make my Mommy better.

That makes me very sad.

My Dad is trying to make me happy. Sometimes he lets me help him make dinner.

Sometimes I help him wash dishes and I help him around the house.

I keep my room clean.
(At least I try these things, I **am** still a kid.)

Without him telling me to, I brush my teeth and go to bed on time.

I'm only a kid and this is a lot for me to think about.

I know that it is not my fault for Mom being sick. I also know that there is nothing that I can do to make her better.

My Dad told me that it is OK for me to worry about her.

He said that it's OK to cry when I feel sad and when I miss her.

My Dad still gives me hugs and kisses because he loves me. I love him too.

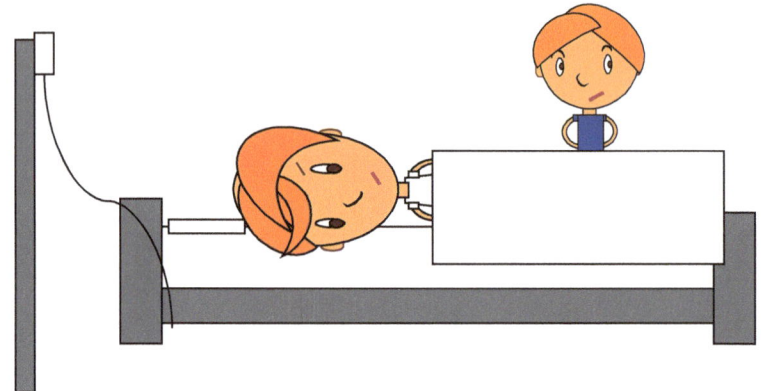

I love my Mommy very much. I hope that she gets better really soon.

I don't want my parents to worry about me. I'm sad but I will be ok.

I will be the best I can be for myself and for them.

That is all that I can do.
And that is OK.

My Life As A Kid

NO TIME FOR ME.

A "TALK TO ME" SERIES BOOK

WRITTEN AND ILLUSTRATED
BY BIRDIE CHESSON

My Mom and Dad are very busy all of the time. I feel like they have no time for me.

I have a babysitter that watches me when my parents are away. They're away a lot.

My babysitter is nice to me.
But she is not my Mom or my Dad.

Even though she cares about me, she cannot love me like my parents do.

I miss my parents so much.

I remember spending time with my parents on weekends and after school.

Now it is just the babysitter and I all of the time.

I'm growing up now. I wonder,
"Do they still know me?"

I don't want them to miss out on all of the things I love to do.
Sometimes, I wish that I could tell them,
"Mom! Dad! I need time with you while I am still young."

I would like to see new things and meet new people together.
I want them to take me to the movies, museums and the zoo. We can build things together. Or we can read books together.

I want them to know that the toys and games that they buy me could never replace them or their love.

I know that I need food, clothes for school and a place to live, so I am not mad at my parents when they go to work. I am grateful for those things.

Even if they had all of the money in the world, all I *really* want them to spend, is time with me.

I want to tell them:

"I love you, Mom. I love you, Dad. I know that you love me too.

Please spend time with me because I <u>really</u> need you in my life <u>*NOW*</u>."

My Life As A Kid

EARL

A Short Play

By Birdie Chesson

EARL

A short play
By Birdie Chesson

A "Talk To Me" Series Story

Dedicated to Earl Pearson
1977-1995

Part 1

It was a nice day today. The sun had finally come out after it rained for five days straight.

I wanted to play outside…badly.

ME: "Mommy, can I go outside and ride my bike?"

MOM: "Are you finished with your homework?"

ME: "Yes Mom."

While I was waiting for my answer from Mom, I stayed in the same spot, looking out of the window. Mom's voice echoed behind me.

MOM: "OK honey, just be back by dinnertime, when the street lights come on."

While watching all of the children playing, my eyes stopped at Earl, a kid from the neighborhood. I see that he is bald headed. I mean, all the way bald.

ME: (Out loud) OK Mom!
(thinking) "That's funny." I said to myself, "Well, last time I saw him, he had a head full of hair."

I went outside. I walked over to him.

ME: "Hey Earl, what happened to your hair?"

EARL looks down.

EARL: "It fell out."

ME: "What do you mean, *fell out*? I mean, **how**?"

He put his head down.
EARL: "I got cancer."

I scratch my head.

ME: "I thought that only grown ups get that."

Earl spoke up.

EARL: "Nope, kids get it too. When I was in the hospital, there were a lot of kids like me in there."

ME: "Wow. Earl, does it hurt?"

EARL: "Yes, it does. But my mommy stayed with me, and I made lots of friends. We were there for each other when one of us felt sicker than the rest of us,. There were some really hard days. But the doctors told me that I am in remission, and that means, I'm OK. So I'm home now."

*I saw that Earl was just like me.
Earl is a kid that likes to have fun and play.
He went to school, did his homework and had a family that loved him.*

*Yes. He was like me.
Everyone wanted him to get better.
I wanted him to get better.*

ME: "Well, Earl, I am glad that you are home. Do you want to ride our bikes together?"

Earl smiled.

EARL: "Oh yeah!"

He grabbed his bike and rode ahead of me.

And we played together until dinnertime, every day.

Earl pt. 2

Earl and I have been best friends for quite awhile now.
We go to school together, do our homework together and play sports together.

One day, while outside playing basketball, I saw that Earl was not feeling well.

I made a shot and instead of trying to block me, he sat on the ground, tired. This was weird to me because Earl wins all of the time.

ME: "Earl, are you OK?"

EARL: "I'm fine." Earl said.
Do you mind if I go home now?"

ME: "Yeah sure, I'll walk you home."

Earl picks up his bike and as he begins to ride away, he falls on the ground.

ME: "Earl!" I yell.

I run over to him.

ME: "Now I *know* you're not feeling well."

EARL: "Please don't tell my mom." *Earl pleads,* "Promise me."

ME: "Earl, *NOW* you are scaring me."

EARL: "*Please* just promise me."
Earl's eyes were so sad.

ME: "Ok, Earl. Just let me help you home."

After that day, now when Earl and I went outside to play, Earl just sat around.

He looked sad and tired all of the time, even at school.

Every day, I'd see him looking exhausted, I say to him, "Let's go, Earl."
I walked him home.

Earl wasn't getting better.

I knew that I had to tell my mom.
I got home, and I opened my mouth...

ME: "Mom..."

MOM: "Go wash your hands first," she interrupted.

As I washed my hands, I was thinking. I knew that Earl did not want me to talk to anyone about it, but I knew that something was wrong with him. I walked into the kitchen.

ME: "Mom, I think that Earl is sick again."

MOM: "What?"

ME: "He is always tired and he keeps falling down."

I begin to cry. "I promised that I wouldn't tell on him."

MOM: "Telling me is what makes you a good friend to Earl."

ME: "What if his cancer is back?"

MOM: "Then you might have saved his life."

The next day, I didn't see Earl. He didn't come to school. He wasn't outside. After a few days of not seeing him, I knocked on his door. His mother opened the door. She spoke in a soft voice:

EARL'S MOM: "Earl isn't here, Sweetie."

I put my head down.

ME: (whispering) "Is he in the hospital?"

EARL'S MOM: "Yes, dear."

ME: "Can I see him?"

EARL'S MOM: "Earl would like that. We'd have to ask your mom first, but I don't see why not."

My eyes lit up.

ME: "Thank you. I'll ask her as soon as I get home."

I begin to walk away.
She clears her throat. I turn around.

EARL'S MOM: "Thank you for telling your Mama. I know that it wasn't easy."

After hearing that, I felt good.

ME: "You're welcome."

I got on my bike and went home.
A few weeks later, when I was able to go to the hospital to see Earl, he was bald again.

ME: "Hi, Earl." I said.

He still looked tired.

EARL: (whispering) "Hey,"

ME: "I am sorry for telling, Earl. But I had to tell."

EARL: "It's OK, I shouldn't have asked you to keep that secret."

I looked down.

ME: "Is the cancer back?"

Earl looked at me.

EARL: "Yes."

I wanted to cry, but I didn't want Earl to feel bad. My eyes hurt but I walked closer to Earl.

ME: "Will you be OK?"

Earl smiled.

EARL: "I will get better, just watch!"

I pat him on the shoulder. I said seriously:

ME: "I care about you Earl. You're my best friend and I hope you feel better soon…
(after a slight pause)
So that I can finally beat you in basketball."

We both laughed. I started to walk towards the door.

EARL: "Hey!" *He shouted.* "Hold this for me."

He grabbed his basketball by the bed and threw it to me. I caught it and smiled.

ME: "It's safe with me, Earl. It will be waiting for you when you come back."

I left the hospital. I was so happy that I saw him. He is my best friend and he needs me to be there for him.

So I will…be there for Earl.

Earl pt. 3

*I wished that the sun was shining but it was raining outside today.
And I wished that I could ride my bike over to my best friend Earl's house.
But he was still in the hospital.
So I just laid on my bed, and stared at the ceiling.*

*I looked over the basketball that Earl gave me.
I thought of my promise to take care of it for Earl until he came back.*

My mother walked into my room.

MOM: "I have to talk to you."

I sit up.
ME: "Yes, Mom?"

MOM: "It's about Earl."

ME: "Yes?"

She looks down.

MOM: "He is gone."

I stand up.

ME: "What do you mean, Mom? Gone?"
I begin to cry. "Gone, Mom?"

She walks over to me. She gives me a hug.

Tears are in her eyes as she holds me. She whispers:

MOM: "Yes Sweetie, Earl is gone."

ME: "You mean that I won't see him again?"

MOM: "No, Dear."

I cry harder. I slowly pull away from my mother.

ME: "Can I be alone?"

MOM: "Are you sure?"

ME: "Yes Mom, I need to be alone."

She looks me in my eyes.
MOM: "Ten minutes, and I'll be back to check on you."

ME: "OK."

I begin to cry again. I walk over on my shelf to see the ball that Earl gave me. I take it into my arms, curled into a ball and fell asleep.

The next morning, my mother took me to Earl's house.

I wanted to say goodbye.
Earl's mother is sitting down, holding his little brother.

Her eyes are red from crying.

Looking at me, she gets up.
She walks over to me, she gives me a hug.
I tried to hand her the ball that Earl gave me.

She looked into my eyes.
EARL'S MOM: "You were Earl's best friend. He wanted you to have it."

ME: "Thank you."
I take a deep breath.

She hugged me tight.

EARL'S MOM: "That hug is from Earl."

ME: "Thank you."

That hug made me feel good.

*As my mother and I walked home,
I sobbed quietly, wiped my eyes and held my head high.*

Sometimes I still cry. I ride my bike everyday. Play basketball. I do all of the things that Earl loved to do.

Even though I am still sad, Earl would not want me to stay home and cry all of the time.

*I still have the ball that he gave me.
I promised that I would keep it safe. So I always will.
I miss Earl so much.*

I think of my best friend Earl and what he meant to me. And how I enjoyed all of the times we had.

Earl's memory is with me and I will never forget him.

My Life As A Kid

I Won't Go With Strangers

Birdie Chesson

I WON'T GO WITH STRANGERS

A "TALK TO ME SERIES' BOOK

Miss Birdie's Books, Inc.
All Rights Reserved

My Mom always told me that if I don't know someone, *that* person is a stranger.

While I was playing outside, a nice man asked me if I wanted to play with his dog.

I love dogs and his dog was really cute. I wanted to pet him.

My Mom always says that not everyone is a good person.

So I said to myself, "His dog looks nice, but I don't know that man."

So I turned and walked away as fast as I could.

The next day, it was raining and my friend Ralphie's mom asked me if I wanted a ride home from school.

I only know Ralphie, but not his mom.
So that means that it is NOT OK for me to get into his mom's car.

She is a stranger to *me*.

So being as polite as I could, I told her, "No, thank you."

I walked home alone in the rain instead.

On the way home from school one day, a nice lady wanted to buy me and my friends ice cream cones. I wanted it because I _love_ ice cream and it was a hot day.

My friends took them, but I said, "No, thanks."

The lady told me that it was OK, because she knew my Mom. And she even said her name.

But I remembered what my Mom said.
So I told her, "That's nice that you know my Mom, but Miss, *I* don't know *you*."

Even though I really wanted that ice cream cone, I didn't take it. So I walked away quickly.

Sometimes it is very hard to say no.
Especially when it means that my friends get the things I like and get to do the things I like to do.

But I still say no.

Like the man with the dog, I wanted to pet the dog.

When Ralphie's mom wanted to drive me home, I did not want to walk home alone in the rain.

And on the hot day when that lady wanted to buy my friends and I ice cream, I wanted it.

But I said no because all of those people were strangers.

There are kids that I hear about on the news.

They are gone because someone took them away from their parents.

Someone could take me away from my family and that scares me.

I used to get upset because I thought that my parents didn't want me to have fun.

Now I know that my Mom and Dad want me to be happy and safe.

Because I listen to them and don't go with strangers,
I can come home safely and
kiss them goodnight, *every* night.

My Life As A Kid

You Are So Special To Me.

You Are So Special To Me.

A "TALK TO ME SERIES' BOOK

by Birdie Chesson

Miss Birdie's Books, Inc.
All Rights Reserved

I came home from school today.
I had something on my mind.

"Mommy, What does adopted mean?

"What did you say? She asked.

"I want to know, Mommy. Where do I come from?"

She smiled at me. "Sit down sweetie."
I sat down.

"Me adopting you means that out of other boys and girls, I chose to keep you."

I was confused. "What do you mean, Mom?"

"You are my child because I chose you."

She walked over to the closet and grabbed pictures of me when I was a baby.

I smiled as we looked at the pictures. I was so cute.

She smiled. "You were so beautiful. But when you were born, you were *so* small. The people that had you before me, could not take good care of you."

"Do you mean that they didn't want me?"

"I didn't say that they didn't want you. But they weren't ready to take good care of you, like you deserve. But *I* was ready and I wanted to love you with all of ***my*** heart. And I still do. You belong with me."

Will they come and take me away from you?"

"It is all about you and what is best for you. So, I will make sure that what happens is what is best for you."

I asked, "Do you love me?"

"Of course I love you. You are my baby and you always will be.
And because I chose **you** makes you even more special to **me**."
She kissed my head. "Do you have any more questions?"

"What about kids that aren't chosen by a parent yet? There's a kid in my class that is in foster care."

"Foster children are very special too. They are kids that are not adopted yet. Foster care is where I found you."

"Ok, can I come back to ask you questions when I think of any?"

"Of course. I am here for you."
He hugged me.
"Ok. Now go do your homework."

Talking about this made me smile. I *am* special anyway and now I know **<u>another</u>** reason why.

My Life As A Kid

MY BEST FRIEND MARIO

MY BEST FRIEND MARIO

Written and Illustrated by
Birdie Chesson
A "Talk To Me" Series Book

I want to tell you about my best friend. His name is Mario.

The day that I met him,
He was eating his lunch alone. I was nervous but I walked over to his table.

"Can I sit with you for lunch?"
I asked.

He said, "Sure."
Mario seemed like a nice boy to me. He asked. "Do you want to share my snack?"

I smiled. "Sure."

After lunch, I asked him, "What happened to your leg?"
He said, "When I was younger, I got sick and the doctors had to take it off."
"Did it hurt?"

"Yes. It hurt a lot. But the pain was more about losing my leg more than the hurt I felt when it was cut off. After awhile, I got used to the pain of losing it and I don't feel it at all now. I'm used to using the chair now."

The bell rang and lunch was over.
I asked, "Can we play some time?"
"I would like that." said Mario.

As I was walking home,
There were kids in the park that were shouting at me.

"Hey you! You and your friend in the wheelchair, how do you play with him?"

"Yeah you probably talk all of the time. He can't do anything!"

I shouted, "He can do anything that you both can do *better*!"

I said it but I wasn't really sure. All I knew was that Mario was a good person that should have friends.

I wanted to be his friend.

When I got home, I could not stop thinking about Mario. My mother saw my face.
"What is wrong, sweetie?"
I told her all about Mario and what happened with the kids at the park today.
"Mario is really nice. But I don't know how to play with him without him having a leg."

My Mom said, "Your heart is in the right place. Find out what Mario likes to do and play that. Keep being a good friend to him. He needs you to be kind and fair with him."

"You're right, Mom. Can I call him?"
"Sure. After you finish your homework."

When I called Mario, I asked him, "What do you like to do?"
I said, "I like video games and I'm really good at basketball."
"Basketball? You play in your wheelchair?"
"Yes I can. It's not hard, it's like most things; With a lot of practice, it's all possible."
"Wow, I'd love to play basketball with you!"
"Good. I'll meet you on the open basketball court at 1 o'clock."
"I'll be there!"
I was so excited. I don't know what will happen but I will play fair.

Mario beat me in two games. He made so many baskets, I lost count! I was out of breath.

Mario said, "Can I tell you something?"

"Sure. Anything!" I said.

"I'm working really hard to walk again."

"That's great! But how?"

"I go to a place that helps me practice walking. I walk and run with a leg that was made just for me. I'll even be able to ride a bike soon."

"Wow Mario! That's great news!"

My friend Mario is special to me.

He is a good friend. He is nice and funny. He is also very smart and does well in school.
We still share lunch everyday.

It has been a few years since we first met and Mario can still play anything and he's good at everything!

Now that he is walking and running on his new leg, everyone wants Mario on their team.

They see how special he really is now, But I knew all along...

My Life As A Kid

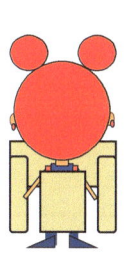  

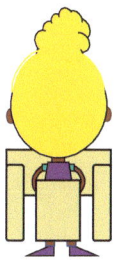 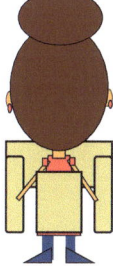

What is under your clothes?

Written and Illustrated by
Birdie Chesson
A "Talk To Me" Series Book

Today, in school we started to talk about our bodies.
After Ms. Smith finished talking about our body parts, she said, "No one should ever touch your bodies. It is your body!"

It made me think of when my mom told me to not let someone see or touch my body.

Then Ms. Smith gave us pages to read.

Our whole class began reading stories about different children that wanted to keep their bodies safe too.

"A girl named Angie was playing with her cousin and he started to touch her in her private places. She didn't want him to and she asked him to stop but he kept touching her anyway. He said that he would hurt her if she told anyone."

"Michael had an uncle that would touch him at while his parents were at work. He wanted his uncle to stop but he kept doing it anyway. The uncle told him not to tell and it was their secret."

"Sally's mother's boyfriend would come into her room at night and would sleep in her bed while her mother was asleep. She didn't want him in her bed. He told her that her mom would be mad if she told on him."

"Marcus had a friend that wanted to be more than friends. The friend was telling him that they loved him and wanted to touch him but Marcus knew that he was too young to make decisions like letting someone touch his body. His friend started to try to force Marcus into it."

"A group of boys wanted Jasmine to send pictures of herself to them. They said that they would like her more and be nicer to her if she did it. Jasmine wanted the boys to be nice to her but she knew that she was too young to show her body to them, so she knew that it was wrong."

"Britney met a friend online.
She thought that her parents didn't care about her friends and the things that she was interested in." Her online friends wanted to meet her somewhere secret so that they could show her another kind of friendship that made her feel good about herself.
Britney knew deep down that there was something different about these friends but they showed her the attention she wanted. Britney also knew that the strangers weren't supposed to make her keep secrets that she couldn't tell her family, so Britney didn't go with the friends that she met. She decided to talk to different adult from another place that she trusted."

After we read the stories, Ms. Smith told us that when it comes to our bodies that there is no such thing as good secrets, that our bodies belong to **only** us and no one has any right to touch us or even ask see our bodies because they are not supposed to, not even friends and family.

I started to think of the kids in these stories and I raised my hand to ask, "So what if something happens to us like the kids in these stories? What do we say and do, Ms. Smith?"

"You say NO! Because NO MEANS NO! You may be afraid but you have to tell an adult that you trust, like me.

If that adult that you tell, tells you to still keep that bad secret, then tell different adult.
There are no such thing as keeping a bad secret. You have to tell **<u>someone</u>** that will finally hear you and you will get help from somewhere.
Your body is *your body*!
Class, let's read the board together."

Our class read the board out loud.

1. No secrets!
2. It's <u>my</u> body!
3. No Means No!

We felt very powerful after we said that.

About My Life As A Kid

My Life as a Kid from Birdie Chesson

My Life as a Kid is from Miss Birdie's Books, Inc.'s original "Talk to Me" Series. The original stories were published in 1998 and were illustrated in 2006.

This is the original cover of the collection in the series. Later, when I started to illustrate, I still wanted to use my son's face, so made I made a cartoon-like version, which is the small colorful picture on the back of this book.

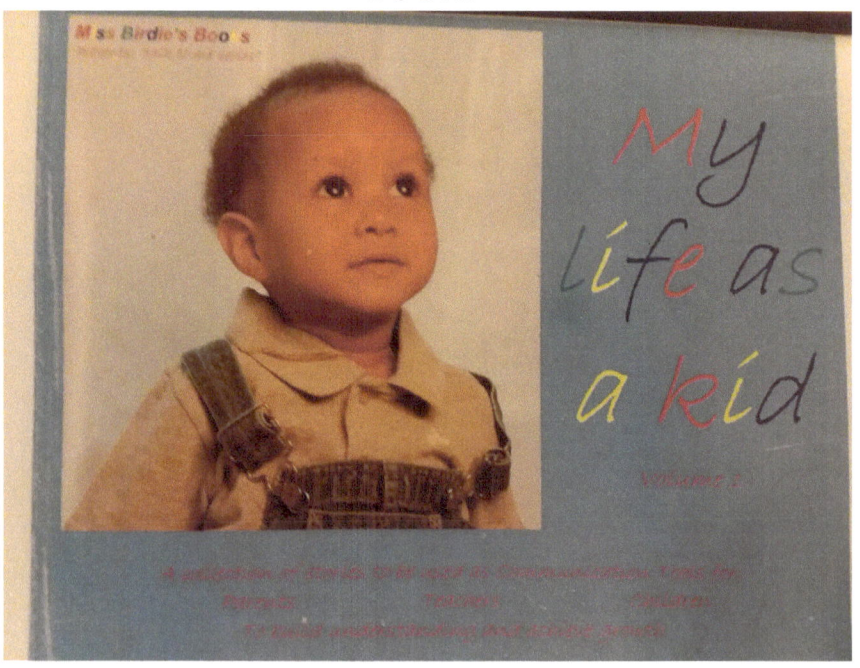

The boy on the cover is Birdie's son, Bam at 2 years old.

My Life as a Kid (cont'd)

The series of stories started when I was a babysitter/nanny in 1997. The children were happy and full of love, but troubled. They were going through things that they couldn't talk to their parents about and they only felt comfortable with talking to me.

So I started writing short stories on the subject and would read it to the children, then leave it behind for the parents to read, in the hopes that there would be a much-needed discussion.

For the most part, my idea was successful but some parents were resistant and in those cases their children still had me to talk to. But I was not their parent.

When my niece and son were born, I wanted them to be able to have open and honest conversations about the things that they were going through. It was important that I'd leave them a legacy.

My Life as a Kid (cont'd)

As my son got older, I used the stories as waiting room material at his schools for the same purpose, wanting families to communicate with each other.

All I can hope is that reading these stories and seeing that there are REAL children that have went through the same things as they or their peers went through is helpful for their mental and emotional development.

All of these stories are based on real children that I've known. I hope that there is true comfort in knowing that.

More…

Are you interested in booking a Workshop, Seminar, Public Appearance or Conference with Birdie Chesson?

Most Popular Workshops:
Momtrepreneurs
Girl Power
Entrepreneur Love
Let's Write a Book!

Birdie Chesson can also insert your mission statement within her message for your group or organization.

Interested in having Birdie host your next event?

Leave a voice message at 914-933-7433
And/or email Birdie at
BookCoachBirdie@gmail.com

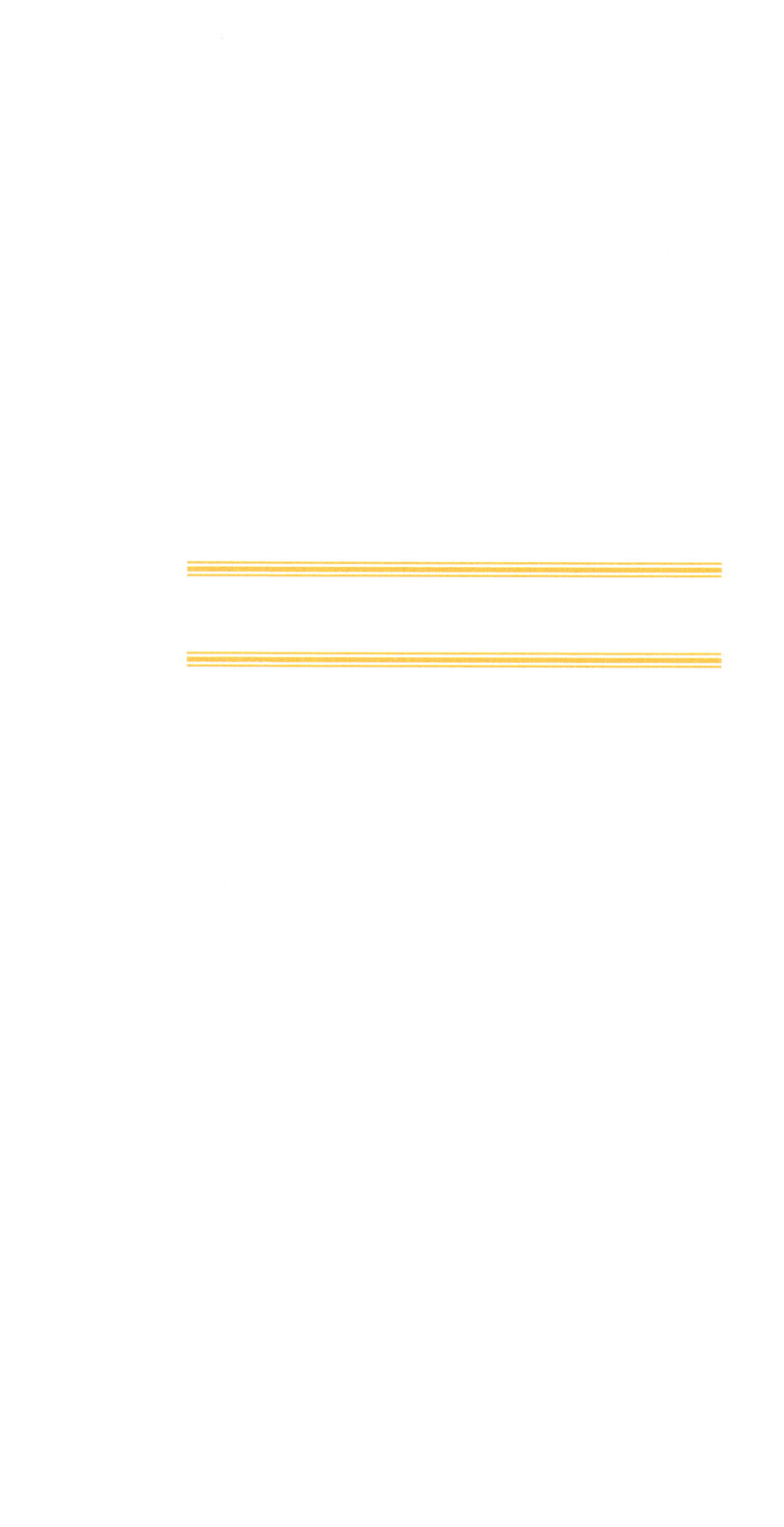

About the Foreword Author

Clint Fisher has had a long career in education. He received his Bachelor of Arts degree in 2002 and immediately moved to Central America where he immersed himself in both the culture and the language. He returned to the states and earned a Master of Science in Education with an emphasis in Guidance Counseling.

This launched a career that has taken him through private and public schools from rural Ohio to the public schools of New York City.

In 2012, Clint also received his clinical counseling license and is recognized as a professional mental health therapist. As a result of his training and experiences, Clint takes an approach with students that is solution focused. He uses various therapeutic and mindfulness techniques to promote an attention to the present moment and reduce emotional reactivity. Outside of school, Clint enjoys a multitude of different activities. He is an avid runner and yogi and recharges by hanging out at home or exploring the city with his partner in crime Adam and their dog Carlos.

About the Author and Illustrator

Birdie Chesson is the author, illustrator and publisher to all of her books. She is also a lifestyle coach helping others find quality of life and as a book coach, she teaches others how to write their own books through her coaching workshops and seminars with over 20 years experience as a public speaker and a leading figure in character development. Birdie is a multiple momtrepreneur that enjoys singing, writing music and scripts for her own independent films.
She is the mother of a son, Bam.

To find out more about her, visit:
www.BirdieChesson.com

www.ingramcontent.com/pod-product-compliance
Lightning Source LLC
Chambersburg PA
CBHW040456240426
43665CB00037B/12